Alexander the Great

FIONA BEDDALL

Level 4

Series Editors: Andy Hopkins and Jocelyn Potter

Pearson Education Limited
Edinburgh Gate, Harlow,
Essex CM20 2JE, England
and Associated Companies throughout the world.

ISBN: 978-1-4058-8206-4

First published by Penguin Books 2004
This edition first published by Pearson Education Ltd 2008

3 5 7 9 10 8 6 4 2

Text copyright © Fiona Beddall 2004
Illustrations by Virginia Gray (Graham-Cameron Illustration)

The moral right of the author has been asserted

Typeset by Graphicraft Ltd, Hong Kong
Set in 11/14pt Bembo
Printed in China
SWTC/02

Published by Pearson Education Ltd in association with
Penguin Books Ltd, both companies being subsidiaries of Pearson Plc

For a complete list of the titles available in the Penguin Readers series please write to your local
Pearson Longman office or to: Penguin Readers Marketing Department, Pearson Education,
Edinburgh Gate, Harlow, Essex CM20 2JE, England.

Contents

Introduction

Alexander cried when Anaxarchus talked about the number of worlds beyond the stars. He explained his tears: 'There are so many worlds, and I have not yet conquered even one.'

Alexander became king of Macedonia 336 years before the birth of Christ, at the age of twenty. Within ten years, he was the ruler of the biggest empire that the world had ever seen. His lands stretched from Greece in the west to India in the east, covering nearly two million square kilometres.

But Alexander died when he was only thirty-two. He had no chance to rule the empire that he had created so quickly.

He was very successful and very young. The great Roman general Julius Caesar lived three centuries later. He read about Alexander and cried, because at the age of thirty-two Caesar had achieved nothing and Alexander had conquered an empire.

About three-quarters of a million Asians lost their lives because of Alexander's great march east. In many lands, he is remembered as a bloodthirsty murderer, not as a conquering hero. But he made close friends as well as enemies among the people that he conquered. He married three Asian women, and filled his army and his court with Asian men. He believed that a mix of Greek and Asian traditions could create a strong empire that would continue for many years.

Alexander's empire did not, in fact, last long. But he joined East and West for the first time, and after this, ideas spread more freely between countries. Although he lived more than 2,300 years ago, Alexander the Great shaped the world that we live in today.

The Empire of Alexander the Great

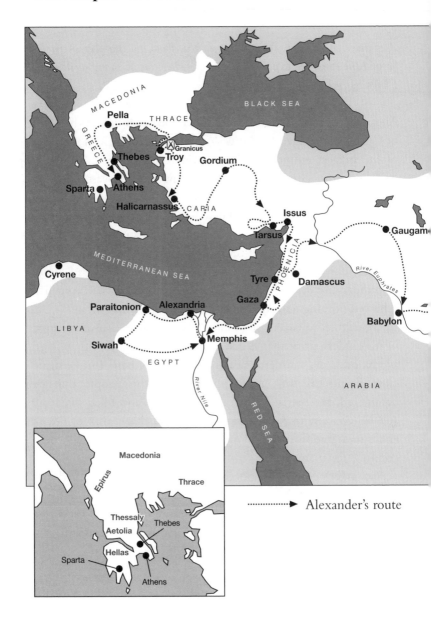

Alexander's route

Chapter 1   The Greek World

On his black warhorse Bucephalas, Alexander, king of Macedonia, rode at the head of his army. Unlike most of his soldiers, he had no beard. His skin was fair and his light-coloured, wavy hair grew long and low on his neck. He was in India, and proud of the past few years. Finally, he had proved that he was the greatest general in history. And he now ruled the greatest empire that the world had ever seen.

His soldiers had joined him from many parts of the world. There were Thracians, Macedonians and Greeks from southeastern Europe; Scythians, Bactrians and Sogdians from central Asia; and Indians, riding their enormous, armoured war elephants. It seemed that no one could stop the march of this extraordinary army. Certainly not the Persians, who had once ruled much of Asia but were now completely defeated by Alexander the Great.

Two centuries earlier, the Persians' enemy in Europe was Greece, not Macedonia. In those days, and during Alexander's lifetime, Greece was not a country. It was a collection of independent city-states which shared a language, a religion and a way of life. Athens and Sparta were two of the most famous city-states, but there were almost 1,500 others. They were not only found in the area that we call Greece today. Greek people lived in coastal areas all around the Mediterranean and the Black Sea. Naples in Italy, Marseille in France and Izmir in Turkey all started life as Greek city-states.

By 500 BC*, the Greek city-states in Asia had lost their independence. They were under the control of the Persian Empire and had to pay high taxes to the Persian king, Darius I. In 499 BC,

* BC: before the birth of Christ

1

they fought for their independence, with the help of the Athenians. Unfortunately, they suffered a serious defeat.

As punishment for this trouble-making, Darius decided to conquer the whole of present-day Greece. In 490 BC, he sent an enormous army to Athens, but the Athenians defeated it at the Battle of Marathon. After the battle, a messenger called Pheidippides ran straight home to Athens to tell everyone the good news. From Marathon to Athens was a distance of 42.195 kilometres – the same distance is called a 'marathon' today in memory of that great run.

When King Darius died, his son Xerxes continued the war against Greece. In 480 BC he sent another army, even larger than his father's one. It defeated the Spartans at Thermopylae (which means 'Gates of Fire') and marched towards Athens. The Athenians had to leave their city to escape the Persian army. While the Athenians were away, the Persians destroyed the buildings on the Acropolis, the religious part of the city. To the Greeks, this was unforgivable.

But the Greeks soon made the Persians pay for their crimes. Athenian ships beat the Persians at sea in the Battle of Salamis, and then the armies of all Greece fought side by side to defeat the Persians at Plataea. Soon the Persian army returned to Asia. The danger had passed. But the Greeks never forgot that they had nearly become part of the Persian Empire.

Although they had fought together in the Persian Wars, the city-states continued to be independent from each other. Some were ruled by a king, or a small group of noblemen. Others, like Athens, were democracies and were ruled by the people. Unlike our democracies today, the ordinary people made all the political decisions. At least forty times a year, they came together in enormous numbers to discuss and vote on matters of government – whether to go to war, when to have public holidays, or how to reduce the number of accidents at sea. Women could not vote, but the ordinary men of these Greek democracies had real power.

Religion was an important part of Greek life. There were many Greek gods. Zeus was the king of the gods, and he used thunder and lightning to punish the people on earth and send messages to them. He had many children, and they too were gods. His son Dionysus was god of the forces of nature; his daughter Athene was connected with learning; and there were many more.

All over the Greek world, people used to visit special places to ask the gods for advice. They asked whether they should start a new business or choose a wife; as city officials, they asked whether they should build a new temple or go to war. Communicating through religious officials, the gods gave them complicated answers that could often be understood in different ways.

In the sixth century BC, for example, the Athenians sent officials to the Greeks' most important religious centre, Delphi. They asked the god Apollo how they should protect themselves from attack by the Persians, and were told that they would be safe from the Persians behind a wall of wood. After much discussion, the Athenians decided that the 'wall of wood' meant ships. They built warships and learnt to sail them. A few years later, they defeated the Persians at sea.

The Greeks believed that the greatest heroes, like Hercules, went to live with the gods when they died. Ordinary people went to a dark place below the earth called the Underworld.

Each Greek city-state was under the protection of one or more of the gods. Each of these gods usually had a temple, built in a style that has been copied in the Western world for almost 2,500 years. To keep their gods happy, the people of the city held regular religious celebrations. They brought gifts, and performed special songs and dances.

The Greeks are remembered for their love of the theatre, which they performed in celebration of the god Dionysus. The plays of great writers like Euripides are still performed today. Other forms of literature were popular too. *The Iliad* and *The Odyssey* by Homer were long poems which told stories about the heroes of the Trojan War. Other Greeks wrote beautiful love poems and the Western world's earliest works of history.

Philosophy was invented in Greece, and the work of Plato and Aristotle is still important today. The Greeks also made many discoveries in mathematics and science. Hippocrates, a doctor of the fifth century BC, is now called 'the father of medicine'. Medical students all over the world have to promise to follow his rules for looking after patients.

The Greeks thought it was important to exercise both their minds and their bodies. They were great admirers of physical beauty in men as well as women. The social centre of a typical Greek city was its gymnasium, where rich citizens took physical exercise. Every four years, the city-states sent their best sportsmen to the city of Olympia for the Olympic Games. There, competitions were held in running, jumping, fighting, horse-riding, chariot racing and spear throwing. The greatest sportsmen at the Olympic Games became heroes of the Greek world, and were celebrated in poems by writers like Pindar.

But the competition between Greek city-states was not always peaceful. There were often wars too. Except in Sparta, Greek armies did not have professional soldiers; the soldiers were usually farmers. Fighting took place in the summer months, and the soldiers went home in the autumn to look after their fields. The wars were usually about land. No city wanted other cities to control too much land or become too powerful. At the end of the fifth century BC, Athens and Sparta were at war for twenty-seven years. It was a time of great suffering all over the Greek world.

At that time, Macedonia in the north was not an important part of Greece. In fact, most Greeks did not think that Macedonia was part of Greece at all. The Macedonians spoke a strange form of

Greek that other Greek speakers had difficulty understanding. Macedonian noblemen liked horse-riding, hunting, eating meat and drinking wine. They did not share other Greeks' interest in literature, science and philosophy.

Macedonia was ruled by a royal family that believed they were relatives of the great god Zeus. The king lived in Pella, Macedonia's capital city. The palace was as beautiful as the finest buildings in Greece, and the Macedonian kings wanted their country to be more Greek. They welcomed several important Greeks there, including many who were escaping the wars. The writer Pindar and the doctor Hippocrates were guests of the Macedonian kings, and Euripides wrote one of his greatest plays in Pella.

And then, in 359 BC, Alexander's father Philip became king, and Macedonia's relationship with the rest of Greece changed for ever.

Chapter 2   A Macedonian Prince

Although Alexander's achievements were extraordinary, in many ways his father, King Philip, was responsible for his success.

When Philip became king of Macedonia, he threw all his energy into increasing his power. He conquered the lands east of Macedonia, which were rich in gold. With this gold, he was able to pay for a full-time, professional army, which gave him a great advantage over the part-time armies of the Greek city-states to his south. It was a well-trained, well-organized army, and soon it had defeated all Macedonia's neighbours. When he died, Philip's empire covered most of modern-day Macedonia, Greece, Albania, Bulgaria and European Turkey.

In Macedonia, men were allowed to have more than one wife at the same time. Philip had six wives. His first wife, his queen and the mother of Alexander, was called Olympias. Olympias was a princess from the neighbouring state of Epirus. She had a strong character and a quick temper. If she had a serious argument with someone, that person was unlikely to stay alive for long. There were many stories about her wild behaviour and her love of the god Dionysus. In the Greek world it was normal to kill a few animals as gifts to the gods. But when Olympias organized religious celebrations, thousands of animals were killed as gifts to Dionysus; then Olympias and her friends drank the animals' blood. They played with poisonous snakes too; it was said that Olympias liked to sleep with a snake in her bed.

It is not surprising, with parents like this, that Alexander was brave and adventurous. His teachers too helped to make him a strong and successful leader. His first teacher was a relative of Olympias – a man called Leonidas. Alexander hated him. Leonidas made Alexander exercise without having breakfast, and gave him only a small snack for his evening meal. He even checked Alexander's school bags, so Olympias could not hide food in them.

Alexander loved music and literature, but his favourite hobby was hunting. He hunted with dogs, and he was always fond of them. Many years later he even named a city in India after his pet dog Peritas. A hunter also needed a horse, and Alexander's horse was one of the most famous in history. A Greek friend of Philip bought it for an enormous sum of money and gave it to Philip as a present. Alexander, aged twelve, went with his father to see this gift. It was a powerful black warhorse, but it was wild. It jumped and kicked and turned. Nobody was able to ride it. When Philip ordered his men to take the horse away, Alexander asked his father to wait. He turned the horse towards the sun, so it could not see its own shadow. It immediately became less frightened. Whispering in its ear, Alexander gently climbed on the horse's back and rode it proudly round the field. Everyone was full of admiration. Philip, it was said, had tears in his eyes as he watched his smiling son. Alexander kept the horse, which he called Bucephalas, and for the next twenty years man and horse were rarely separated.

He turned the horse towards the sun.

As Philip became richer and more powerful, he hired philosophers, artists, musicians and engineers from all over the Greek world. His court at Pella was an exciting place for a young prince to grow up. Alexander could talk to people who had lived in Egypt, and made friends with a man who had been a governor in the Persian Empire. Macedonia was now well-connected in the wider world.

Philip was too busy leading his army to spend much time with his son. But he made sure that Alexander's teacher during his teenage years would be the best that money could buy. When Alexander was thirteen, his father hired Aristotle, a student of the great philosopher Plato. At that time, Aristotle was an unknown teacher with thin legs and small eyes. He also had one of the sharpest and most questioning minds in history. Aristotle later wrote many important works of philosophy. He was one of the first people to use scientific methods to learn more about plants and animals. He studied the stars and the way that the sea shapes the land. He wrote about politics and literature. The list of his interests and achievements is extraordinary.

Nobody knows how much he taught Alexander. Aristotle later wrote that it was a waste of time teaching political science to a young man, because 'he has no experience of life, and still follows his emotions'. Was he describing his pupil Alexander here? Perhaps. But as Alexander grew up, like his teacher he never stopped asking questions. Whenever Pella had visitors from other parts of the world, Alexander learnt as much as he could from them. Alexander, like Aristotle, had a hunger for knowledge.

Alexander was not Aristotle's only pupil in Macedonia. Aristotle also taught the sons of leading noblemen, and among them were many of Alexander's future commanders: Ptolemy, Perdiccas, Seleucus, Nearchus, and Alexander's best friend Hephaistion. These friends, like the horse Bucephalas, followed Alexander loyally to the ends of the earth.

Alexander grew up quickly into a responsible and intelligent young man. When he was sixteen, he was allowed to take charge of the government while Philip was away with the army. Soon after this, a tribe to the east of Macedonia started to cause trouble, and Alexander himself led a small army to defeat it. Then, when he was eighteen, he commanded part of his father's great army at the Battle of Chaeronea. In this battle the Macedonians finally defeated the Greek city-states and forced them to accept Philip as their leader.

Philip started to make plans to free the Greek cities in Asia from Persian rule. Alexander felt that he would have an important part to play in his father's war against Persia. The future looked good. But then his father fell in love.

Eurydice was the daughter of a Macedonian nobleman. She was young and very beautiful. Soon Philip was planning their wedding.

Olympias was very angry because, as Philip's new wife, Eurydice would be more powerful than she was. And if Eurydice had a son, he could be chosen as king instead of Alexander. At the wedding, there was a big argument. Alexander attacked his father, although no one was hurt. Alexander and his mother left the court immediately; Alexander soon returned, but his mother went to live in her home country, Epirus.

Without his mother, Alexander was very nervous about his position at court. Then he heard news that made him even more worried. In preparation for his war on Persia, Philip was in contact with the king of Caria, on the western edge of the Persian Empire, and the two rulers wanted to arrange a family marriage. As well as Alexander, Philip had another son, Alexander's half-brother Arrhidaeus. He had learning difficulties and could never be given adult responsibilities. Philip suggested that Arrhidaeus should marry a Carian princess.

Alexander could not understand why his father wanted this

royal marriage for Arrhidaeus and not for him. He sent friends to the Carian court to say that he would make a much better husband than his half-brother. The Carian king was pleased at first. But Philip was very angry when he heard what Alexander had done. He did not want to waste Alexander on a small country like Caria. Alexander's friends were sent away from Macedonia, and soon the Carian king got worried and lost interest in a marriage with anyone in Philip's family. Alexander had ruined everything. His position at court became even weaker than before.

As Philip sent part of his army into Asia to start the war against Persia, he planned another wedding. Cleopatra, Alexander's sister, was marrying her uncle, the king of Epirus. All the local rulers in Philip's empire were there. But Olympias, who was Cleopatra's mother as well as the king of Epirus's sister, was not at the wedding. Since he was joining the royal families of Epirus and Macedonia with this new marriage, Philip did not need Olympias and her Epirote connections.

After the wedding, Philip was walking to the celebrations with Alexander and his daughter's new husband. His endless battles had left him with one eye and a bad leg, but he was still full of energy, dreaming of a successful war in Persia. Suddenly, a man moved towards them. It was one of Philip's bodyguards. Without a word, he pushed a knife into Philip's chest.

Then he ran. But he fell as he tried to get on his horse, and Philip's other bodyguards soon killed him.

There was no hope for King Philip. He was dead.

Chapter 3   The Young King

We will never know why Philip was killed. He certainly had many political enemies inside and outside his empire who had the money to pay for his murder. Some people at the time said that

Philip and his murderer had argued about a lover. But it is more likely that Olympias was responsible. Philip had not included his first wife in his plans for Macedonia's great future, so Olympias, quick-tempered and dangerous, had arranged his murder. She would have more power as King Alexander's mother than as King Philip's unwanted wife.

But in Macedonia, rule did not always pass to the dead king's oldest son. At the time of his father's murder, many people did not want Alexander as their king. He was still only twenty – too young, they said, to take on the responsibility of Macedonian rule. He was half Epirote, not a true Macedonian, because his mother was from Epirus. And his Epirote mother was wild and irresponsible – perhaps even her husband's murderer.

There were two other serious possibilities for the next king. One was General Attalus, Eurydice's uncle, who wanted to rule Macedonia through Eurydice and Philip's new baby son. The other was Amyntas.

Twenty-three years earlier, Amyntas had been a child of two when his father, King Perdiccas, had died. Philip was Perdiccas's younger brother and had ruled in the place of his baby nephew; when Amyntas became an adult, Philip was so powerful and successful that nobody questioned his right to continue ruling. Amyntas was now twenty-five. Compared to Alexander, he had the advantage of age and experience, and his blood was equally royal. He was popular with the noblemen of Macedonia.

But Alexander stayed one step ahead of his enemies. He ordered the murder of Eurydice's baby, his own half-brother. General Attalus, who was with the army in Asia, could do nothing to stop him. Soon Attalus and Amyntas were murdered too. This was not unusual – in those days the rule of a new king almost always started with a few murders. Alexander reduced taxes for the people of Macedonia and, since no other suitable kings were left alive, they seemed happy to accept him as their new ruler.

The situation was more difficult abroad. When news of Philip's murder spread around his empire, the tribes in the north and the city-states in the south decided to free themselves from Macedonian rule. Within a few months of his father's death, Alexander had to fight to keep the empire together.

He first went to the Greek state of Thessaly. The usual route was along a narrow valley in the mountains, but this was now guarded by the Thessalians. Alexander decided that it was too dangerous to take the Macedonian soldiers and warhorses this way. Instead, he created a new path. He ordered the soldiers to cut steps in the steep rockface of a mountain on the border between Macedonia and Thessaly. After weeks of hard work, his army entered Thessaly by the new road, took the Thessalians by surprise and defeated them easily. The Thessalians welcomed Alexander as their new leader.

A march at lightning speed then took Alexander's army on a tour of Greek city-states. One by one, they realized that battle would end in disaster, so they quickly made peace with him instead. Only Sparta refused to accept Alexander as their leader, sending the message: 'It is our fathers' habit not to follow others but to lead them.' Alexander was not too worried. The rest of the Greeks hated Sparta more than they hated Macedonia. He could manage without Spartan help.

There were also problems in the north. After his tour of Greece, Alexander had to fight the Thracians, who lived beside the River Danube. They could not defeat Alexander's well-trained army and soon they were forced to accept Macedonian rule.

But bad news followed. The Macedonian forces in Asia were retreating; Attalus, murdered on Alexander's orders, had been a good general, and his death had probably weakened the army there. In Macedonia itself, Olympias was behaving typically and had murdered Eurydice. And in Greece, news was spreading that Alexander had been killed on the Danube; the city-state of Thebes was leading a new fight for independence which was fast growing out of control.

Alexander knew that he had to act quickly. He rushed his army to Thebes and started a siege of the city. When an unguarded gate in the city wall was found, the Macedonians soon forced their way into the city.

Alexander called a meeting with the neighbouring Greek city-states, who had for many years suffered bad treatment at the hands of power-hungry Thebes. When he asked them what should happen to Thebes, they voted to destroy it completely.

Thebes came to a violent end. The city's riches were taken. A few houses were left untouched – 150 years earlier the Theban writer Pindar had written poems for the Macedonian king, and now his house was safe – but the rest were burnt to the ground. 30,000 Thebans, including women and children, were taken prisoner and sold as slaves.

The terrible news soon spread around Greece. No other city-state was interested in continuing their fight for independence now. Everyone rushed to prove that they were Alexander's greatest allies.

At last Alexander could turn his attention to Asia. It was time to plan his war against the Persian Empire.

Alexander called together forces from many lands – foot soldiers from Illyria and Thrace, horsemen from Thessaly, warships from Athens, archers from Crete, as well as the highly trained Macedonian army. To this he added doctors, long-distance runners, engineers, religious men, specialists in digging for gold and jewels, and a historian called Callisthenes to record his great achievements.

Alexander left his mother Olympias in charge of Macedonia, with his father's loyal general Antipater to lead her army. Then he marched to the Dardanelles, a narrow piece of water that separates Europe from Asia in present-day Turkey.

While Alexander's second-in-command, General Parmenion, led the main army into Asia by the shortest sea crossing, Alexander himself decided to see some sights.

His destination was the ruined city of Troy, scene of the legendary Trojan War, where Greeks and Asians had fought for the first time. The Greeks believed that the war had started 1,000 years before the time of Alexander, when Paris, a Trojan prince, stole the beautiful Helen from her Greek husband Menelaus.

♦

Of all the heroes of the Trojan War, the greatest was Achilles. When he was a baby, his immortal mother had held his heel and covered the rest of his body in the water of the legendary River Styx. After this, he could only be hurt on his heel.

Achilles grew up handsome and brave. At the start of the Trojan War, his mother gave him a choice: he could stay at home, live a normal life and die an old man, or he could go to Troy, die young and be famous for ever. Of course Achilles chose Troy.

He was the fastest runner and the strongest fighter in the Greek army. But he also had a quick temper. After an argument about a female prisoner with his general, Agamemnon, Achilles decided to stop fighting in the war. Without Achilles, the Greeks were nearly defeated. Patroclus, Achilles's best friend, fought in Achilles's armour to give the Greeks confidence; but soon he was killed by the Trojan hero, Hector.

Achilles felt very sad and very guilty. It was his fault that his best friend was dead. Dressed in new armour created by the gods, he returned to battle and did not stop fighting until he had killed Patroclus's killer, Hector. He tied Hector's body to his chariot and pulled it through the dust. But later in the war, Achilles himself was killed when Paris shot him in the heel with a poisoned arrow.

♦

This was a story that Alexander had read from his early childhood. He was even thought to be a relative of Achilles, through his mother, Olympias, and the royal family of Epirus. His teacher Aristotle had prepared for him a special copy of *The Iliad*, Homer's great poem about Achilles; this copy was so important to Alexander that he liked to rest his head on it when he slept. For many years people had compared Alexander and his best friend Hephaistion to Achilles and Patroclus. And now Alexander, like the Greeks of the Trojan War, had come across the Dardanelles to attack the people of Asia.

As Alexander's boat touched the beach, he threw his spear at the ground as a sign that this land was now his. With his friends, he walked up the hill to the ruins of Troy. He gave gifts to the gods. Then he and Hephaistion ran – Alexander to the tomb of Achilles, his best friend to the tomb of Patroclus. Next he went to the temple of Athene, where he exchanged his own armour for a shield which, according to legend, had been used in the Trojan War. With his beautiful shield from the Age of Heroes, he went to rejoin his army as the new Achilles. We can only wonder if he thought about the choice of futures that Achilles had been given by his mother. Like Achilles, Alexander chose to fight battles and live famously. Did he guess that, like Achilles, he would never return to his homeland or live to middle age?

Chapter 4   First Battles in Asia

Until Alexander could prove that he was stronger than the Persian Empire, the Greek cities in Asia refused to help him. He had very little food or pay left for his men. He needed to defeat the Persians in battle quickly. But the Persian commanders were discussing other plans.

At this time, the soldiers in the Persian army were mostly Greek.

People talk of Alexander's 'Greeks' defeating the 'Persians', but there were 50,000 Greeks in the Persian army and only 7,000 in Alexander's.

In Greece, it was difficult to earn a living if you did not own land. There were plenty of slaves, so landowners and businessmen rarely wanted to employ paid workers. The shipping business was a possibility, but storms at sea were common and fortunes were lost as often as they were made. For many, the most attractive choice was a life in the highly paid Persian army. The army was full of failed Greek farmers and businessmen, younger sons who owned no land, and politicians who were not welcome in the city of their birth.

A Greek general called Memnon had been responsible for the Macedonians' most recent defeats. He had grown up on the island of Rhodes, spent some time living in Macedonia, and come to Asia fifteen years before Alexander. His wife Barsine was Persian, and he now owned a large farm, a present from the Persian king for his loyal service.

Memnon now had a plan to defeat Alexander. The Persians should not face the Macedonians in battle, he advised. Instead, they should burn their own farms and make sure Alexander's army could get no food. If Alexander did not win a battle, the Greek cities would not help him. Soon his hungry soldiers would have to return to Europe.

The rest of the Persian commanders disagreed with Memnon. Instead, they decided to defend their country in battle.

The Persian army grouped on the east bank of the River Granicus. When Alexander heard the news, he realized his luck and ordered his soldiers to march there as quickly as possible. Some of Alexander's advisers warned him that for religious reasons it was not a good month for a battle. Alexander acted typically: he created a new month.

Alexander and his army reached the Granicus in late afternoon.

Alexander and his army reached the Granicus in late afternoon.

The Persians had chosen their position well. The river was twenty metres wide and ran fast between steep, muddy banks. If Alexander ordered his army to cross the river, it would be easy for the Persians to cut them down in the mud.

Alexander had read in the work of a Greek historian that the Persians liked to camp some distance from their chosen battle ground and did not march before the sun came up. The Macedonians crossed the river in the early hours of the morning and found it undefended. They now had the advantage of surprise.

Alexander led his horsemen against the enemy. The Persian horsemen fought back, but they were badly organized because of the surprise attack. When Alexander's spear broke during the fighting, a Persian commander saw his opportunity and struck Alexander on the head. But Alexander was not hurt, and before the Persian could strike again, a Macedonian called Cleitus came to protect his king. Cleitus's sister had been Alexander's nurse as a baby, and now Cleitus saved his life.

As the fighting continued, the Persians failed to organize a strong defence. Many of their commanders were killed, several by Alexander himself. Soon the Persians on horseback were retreating.

As the Macedonians surrounded the Persian camp, about 17,000 hired Greek foot soldiers tried to defend it. They managed to hurt Alexander's horse, but there were many more Macedonian attackers. They could not hope to win. 2,000 were taken prisoner, and later sent to Macedonia as slaves; the rest were killed. Alexander used this cruel treatment as a message to other Greeks: 'Leave the Persian army and stop fighting your own countrymen – if you don't, your suffering will be worse than the Persians'.'

After his success at the Granicus, the Greek cities in Asia quickly opened their gates to Alexander. He sent messengers to all the cities that he had already passed, telling them to become democracies, to create their own laws, and to stop paying tax to the Persian king. This was a clever trick, because it made Alexander popular with tax-payers. The tax to the Persian king was not really stopped; it was given a new name, and paid as a 'gift' to the Macedonian army instead. But the trick was successful. The Persian-supported local rulers lost their power without any danger to the Macedonian army. The cities became democratic, and Alexander grew so popular that many people in the area started to think of him as a god.

Alexander marched south into Caria, where he had in the past hoped to marry the daughter of his father's ally, the Carian king. At the border, he was met by Queen Ada, who had been the wife of an earlier king. Now she was almost a prisoner in her own home under the new king, a Persian called Orontobates. She had a strange suggestion for Alexander: he should become her adopted son and take Orontobates's place as the true king.

But first he had to defeat King Orontobates. Orontobates and General Memnon, who was then commander of the whole Persian army, were preparing a defence of Halicarnassus (now called Bodrum, in Turkey). The city was famous for its Mausoleum – the great tomb of Ada's brother, King Mausolus, which was one of the Seven Wonders of the World. Halicarnassus had the strongest city defences on the Asian coast, circled by walls and with a well-built castle. Persian warships defended it by sea; Alexander, who had sent his Athenian warships home a few months earlier because they were so expensive, had no warships at all.

The siege was difficult. The Macedonians broke part of the city wall, but the Persians pushed them back. Many lives were lost from both armies. In the end, the Persians had too few soldiers to defend the city. They retreated to the castle, which they held for a year. But Alexander was able to move his forces into the main part of the city. As Queen Ada's adopted son, Alexander became king of Caria.

Preparations now had to be made for the winter. Alexander

decided to send home to Macedonia all the soldiers who had married just before the start of the war. This was a popular decision. Alexander's army now loved their leader more than ever.

Alexander left his 'mother', Queen Ada, in charge of Caria. With the rest of the army, he marched to Gordium (in central Turkey), and waited there for the return of the newly married soldiers. During the winter Alexander became interested in a local legend. In the palace at Gordium, which had in the past been the home of the kings of Phrygia, there was an old chariot. It was tied to a piece of wood by a complicated knot that no one had ever managed to untie. According to legend, Asia would one day be ruled by the person who could untie the knot.

Alexander decided that he would untie the knot. In front of all his soldiers, he moved towards the chariot. After some minutes, the knot was broken. But there were two different stories from the people who were watching. Some said that Alexander's success with the knot was real; others said that they saw him use his knife to cut it. We will never know. But that night the gods seemed to send a sign of their support when thunder and lightning filled the sky. Word spread among his soldiers and the local people: Alexander, who had untied the Gordian Knot, was the future ruler of all Asia.

Chapter 5   Face to Face with Darius

While Alexander was at Gordium, the Persians started to make more plans to defeat him. The Macedonians had no warships; the Persians had 300. It was time for the Persians to take advantage of their power at sea.

Led by General Memnon, they took back the Greek islands of Chios and Lesbos. They planned to continue by sea towards central Greece, and they hoped that Sparta would soon lead a Greek independence movement against the Macedonians. If the Persians created enough problems in Greece, Alexander would have to go home.

They also decided, finally, to burn all the fields before Alexander reached them, so his army would have nothing to eat. Marching south, Alexander found burning fields everywhere. Then, when he got to the city of Tarsus (in present-day southern Turkey), he became ill with a high fever, perhaps because of a swim in an icy river. His doctors feared for his life. But a Greek doctor called Philip, who had looked after Alexander as a boy, suggested a treatment that might help. As the doctor went to prepare the medicine, Alexander was given a letter from General Parmenion, his second-in-command; it said that Philip had been paid by the Persian king to kill Alexander. But when Philip returned with the medicine, Alexander drank it immediately without questioning his doctor's loyalty, and after several weeks he got better. In Alexander's world, death by poison was not uncommon and the ability to know friend from enemy was very useful.

Memnon was not as lucky as Alexander. While fighting on Lesbos, he suddenly became ill and died. This was a serious problem for the Persians. Without Memnon and his knowledge of Greece, they did not feel confident that they could fight a war successfully against the Macedonians in Europe. Although Memnon's plan had worked very well until then, they decided to change it completely.

The Great King of Persia, Darius III, took personal control of the situation. We know little about this king. Although he had royal blood, he was not a close relative of the Persian kings that had ruled before him. He had been the governor of Armenia and fought bravely in battles there; he had then become king of Persia after many members of the royal family were poisoned by a power-hungry politician called Bagoas.

Persia itself was in present-day Iran, but the Great King

21

controlled all the lands from Egypt to Pakistan, and from Uzbekistan to the Arabian Sea. His riches were legendary, and he received the treatment of a god. He was protected by a bodyguard of 10,000 soldiers; they were called the Immortals because when one man died or became ill, his position was immediately filled by another man.

The Great King gave land to the men that served him well. The land-owning Persians had a very comfortable way of life that was often a subject of wonder among the Greeks. They had soft carpets on their floors and beautiful gardens full of flowers; they ate the finest food, and hundreds of servants looked after all their needs. But with one word, the all-powerful king could take away their good fortune for ever.

Wide, well-built roads connected the Great King's most important cities, Babylon, Susa and Persepolis, with the far corners of his empire. The best of these roads was the Royal Road, which led 2,300 kilometres from Susa, in the heart of the empire, to Sardis, on the Mediterranean coast. Every twenty-five kilometres along the route, there was a place to buy food and stay the night.

Only the Greek cities in the west of the Persian Empire paid tax in the form of money. Everywhere else, tax to the Great King was paid in food; in silver and gold; and in horses, war chariots and fighting men. King Darius now put together an enormous army. Only the lands on the eastern borders of the empire did not send men; they were too far away to be useful.

The Persian army's strength lay in its well-trained archers and horsemen, because riding and archery were the traditional hobbies of the Persian landowners. Tens of thousands of these men joined their king, but foot soldiers were less easy to find. Darius's army included a large number of teenage boys with no experience of battle. To help them, the King also called for the hired Greek soldiers who had been fighting with Memnon at sea; he needed them now for a great land battle.

Historians at the time wrote that he had between 300,000 and 600,000 men in his army, but not all of them were soldiers. Each Persian horseman, for example, had twelve servants. And when the king commanded the army, his politicians, his wives and his children came with him.

The Macedonians, whose army only numbered about 50,000 men, received reports that the enemy had camped near the Syrian border with Cilicia (southern Turkey). They marched along the Mediterranean coast towards the Persian camp, covering the distance in half the usual time.

Unknown to Alexander, the Persians had left their camp and were also marching. While the Macedonians followed the coast road south, the Persians followed the inland road north. Although they were only a few kilometres away from each other, neither army knew where the other one was. Such confusion is hard to imagine today, in a world where cameras in space can be used to spy on every movement that an army makes.

The Macedonians realized first that the two armies had passed each other by mistake. They had already had several days of hard marching. Now Alexander asked his soldiers to turn round and march again.

After an evening meal, they marched north in the dark, had a short sleep, then marched again at first light. Around midday they came to a river near the town of Issus. On the far side of the river stood the Persian army, on a flat piece of land about two kilometres wide. To the west there was beach and the Mediterranean Sea; to the east there were mountains. The fighting area was too narrow for Darius to take advantage of his greater numbers of soldiers. It was a good battlefield for the Macedonians.

Alexander, riding Bucephalas, led a charge of horsemen across the river towards the enemy. The Persian horsemen rode to meet them, and the battle began. In the centre of the battlefield were the Macedonian foot soldiers, who fought with six-metre-long spears.

Although they were difficult to defeat on flat ground, the Macedonians were having problems on the steep river banks. They were close to defeat at the hands of the hired Greek soldiers who fought for the Persians.

But just in time, Alexander's horsemen broke through the Persian line and came to help the foot soldiers. Soon the Macedonians were winning the battle.

King Darius was watching the fighting from his chariot. As Alexander and his Macedonian horsemen moved towards him from two sides, the eyes of the two kings met for a moment. Then Darius, realizing that the battle was lost, turned his chariot and quickly retreated.

Chapter 6   South to Egypt

Darius escaped over the mountains on horseback, leaving his spear in his chariot. But the Battle of Issus was a serious defeat for the Persians. Enormous numbers of Persians died. The rest of the Persian army broke into small groups, and most of the hired Greeks sailed home in Persian warships.

King Darius lost much more than his soldiers and ships. The Macedonians found extraordinary riches left near the battlefield, and even more at the city of Damascus. There were 220 kilograms of silver, and as many gold coins as Alexander's father, King Philip, had received in tax from his empire in a whole year. There were piles of cups, bowls and boxes made of gold. Alexander liked one gold box so much that he decided to keep his favourite copy of *The Iliad* in it. There were thousands of servants, including 329 female musicians, 319 cooks and 70 wine waiters, who had come to look after the Great King while he commanded the army. And, most important of all, the Macedonians took prisoner Darius's wife, mother and children.

Darius, realizing that the battle was lost, quickly retreated.

Alexander made sure that the Persian royal family received royal treatment. They were given fine clothes and jewellery to wear, and had a comfortable place to live. Soon Darius wrote to Alexander asking for his family's return. But Alexander replied that the royal family would only be freed if Darius called him King Alexander of Asia.

'If you think you have a right to your empire, stand and fight for it,' wrote Alexander. 'Do not run away, because I will come after you, wherever you go.'

Another prisoner was the dead General Memnon's beautiful Persian wife, Barsine. She had lived for a short time in Macedonia when her father, a Persian governor, had become unpopular with the Persian king. In Macedonia, Barsine had known Alexander as a boy. Now he was a man and she was his prisoner. Alexander fell in love with her and they were close for the next five years.

Alexander now needed to take the ports in Phoenicia (present-day Lebanon). Most of them were happy to welcome the Macedonians and say goodbye to Persian rule, but the city of Tyre was different. Tyre stood on an island about a kilometre out to sea and was ringed by a wall fifty metres high. Few cities were as difficult to attack, but Alexander, as usual, wasted no time in worrying about the difficulty of his job.

He told his engineers to build a wide road across the sea to the island of Tyre. Using stone from coastal ruins to fill in the sea, the first part of this road was built quickly. But the last 200 metres cost many lives.

The Tyrians shot arrows at the Macedonians as they worked, but the Macedonians used stone-throwing machines to clear the archers from their shooting positions. The machines were also used to make holes in the city walls, but the walls were soon rebuilt. When the Tyrians sailed burning ships into enemy lines to destroy the Macedonians' wooden war machines, the Macedonians found other ways to destroy the Tyrian defences. The Macedonians tried to climb the walls, but the Tyrians showered them with red hot sand that poured inside their armour and burnt their bodies horribly.

As time went on, Alexander was helped by other Phoenician cities, and by the Greeks who lived on Cyprus and Rhodes. More than six months after the start of the siege, the Macedonians and their allies attacked the island on all sides with ships and machines of war. Finally, Alexander and his soldiers managed to fight their way over the walls. The Tyrians defended themselves bravely, but the city was taken. 10,000 Tyrians were killed and 30,000 were sold as slaves.

The results of Alexander's siege can still be seen. Tyre exists today, but it is not on an island. The coastline was changed for ever by the road that Alexander's soldiers built across the sea.

South of Tyre, Alexander took the city of Gaza after a two-month siege. The whole male population was killed. Then Alexander tied the feet of their dead king, Batis, to his chariot and pulled it round the city. His hero Achilles had done the same in *The Iliad*, with the body of Patroclus's killer, Hector.

Alexander then marched south to Egypt, a land rich in gold and farmland. In later years, when Rome was all-powerful and had a city population of one million, most of the Romans' food came from the valley of the Nile.

The Egyptians were understandably proud of their long history. Their religion and their writing had begun almost 3,000 years before the time of Alexander, and their form of government had too. The Egyptians had built extraordinary tombs for their kings, or 'pharaohs'. The greatest of these, the tomb of Khufu at Giza, continued to be the tallest building in the world until the nineteenth century. But when it was built in the twenty-sixth century BC, the Greeks had not yet even learnt how to write.

For centuries, Egypt had been one of the most powerful countries in the Middle East, but in 525 BC it had fallen under

Persian rule. Its people had never fully accepted this situation, and had regularly fought for their independence.

Now they welcomed Alexander as their new ruler. They were deeply religious, and they saw that Alexander had a better attitude than the Persian kings to the Egyptian gods. They gladly made him their 'pharaoh'. As Pharaoh, he was believed to be a living god, son of the Egyptian creator-god Amun.

After spending time in Egypt's capital city Memphis (near present-day Cairo), Alexander travelled north to the mouth of the River Nile. There he organized the building of a new city, Alexandria. It was not the only city of that name; one had already been built near Issus, and before he died Alexander built more than twenty others. But this Alexandria was perhaps his greatest gift to the future. In the centuries that followed, it became one of the Mediterranean world's most important centres of learning and of political and economic power.

Leaving most of his army in Alexandria, Alexander travelled 200 kilometres west along the Mediterranean coast with a small group of soldiers. He came to the Greek city of Paraitonion, then turned south into the Libyan desert. This time his destination was not an enemy city – it was Siwah, home of the Libyan god Ammon.

Siwah, in Libya, was known all over the Greek world as a place where people could ask Ammon for advice and receive an honest answer. The answers were communicated to visitors by Ammon's religious officials. Ammon was connected with the Egyptian god Amun and the Greek god Zeus.

It seems that Alexander had an important question to ask the god. But his journey across the desert to Siwah almost cost him his life. For four days the travellers were lost in a sandstorm. They drank all their water and soon became very thirsty. But suddenly there were clouds in the sky and it started to rain – 'not without the help of the gods', according to Alexander's friends. They travelled at night, when it was cooler, and soon they lost their way again. This time, it was said, they were helped by birds and snakes which showed them the right direction. Finally, after more than a week in the desert, they reached Siwah.

Alexander communicated privately with the god Ammon, possibly about his hopes of becoming King of Asia. Later, in public, the religious men of Siwah welcomed him as 'Son of Zeus'. Was this just a Greek translation of the Pharaoh's title, Son of Amun? Or had they heard that Alexander's mother Olympias sometimes told strange stories about a god being her son's father? We do not know. But certainly Alexander's visit to Siwah had a powerful effect on him. According to his soldiers, he started to believe that he truly was the son of the great god Zeus. Like the Greek hero Hercules, he was more than human; because of this, there was nothing that he could not achieve.

Chapter 7   King of Asia

During the siege of Tyre, King Darius had written another letter to Alexander. He had offered him all the lands west of the River Euphrates, a fortune in gold, and marriage to his daughter; in exchange, Darius had asked for peace and the return of his wife, mother and children. It was a generous offer, but Alexander had refused it. Darius then realized that he had no choice – he had to fight again.

While Alexander was in Egypt, Darius called together a new army. Soldiers came from the farthest corners of his empire, and it was a whole year before the army was ready to fight.

Alexander marched from Egypt to Tyre and waited. In his next battle, he wanted to defeat the Persians completely, and he could not do this against an incomplete army. To entertain his bored soldiers, he organized the performance of Greek plays and musical concerts. Then finally the Macedonians marched east.

By burning the Euphrates valley, the Persians forced Alexander to take the only other possible route east. This brought him to Darius's choice of battlefield: Gaugamela, in present-day Iraq.

Darius made sure that, unlike at Issus, the battlefield was wide enough for him to take advantage of his enormous army. Although Alexander had been joined by new soldiers from Macedonia, Greece and the Asian Mediterranean coast, these only took the place of the men who had died. Against Alexander's 7,000 horsemen and 40,000 foot soldiers, Darius's had 30,000 horsemen and 200,000 foot soldiers to send into battle.

At first Alexander planned to take the Persians by surprise in the early morning. But when it became clear that Darius was expecting them, the Macedonians took time to look carefully at the battlefield. In the centre of the field, they saw that spears had been stuck in the ground to hurt any horses that ran at the enemy lines. They saw elephants, a frightening sight for men who had never met such enormous animals before, and for their horses. They also noticed that uneven ground had been flattened to help the drivers of the famous Persian war chariots. Darius had 200 of these chariots, with spears pointing out in front of the horses and long knives fixed to the wheels. It is unlikely that the ordinary Macedonian soldiers were feeling confident before the battle.

The following morning, Alexander spoke to his men and their confidence returned. He called to the gods, 'If I am truly the son of Zeus, you will defend us and help to make us strong.' Then he led the attack.

Horsemen and foot soldiers charged towards the centre of the Persian line, then suddenly turned right to an area where there were no spears or elephants. Darius's horsemen from the centre rushed to meet them, but they were unable to surround the Macedonians as they had hoped. Fighting hard, the Macedonians drove them back.

At the same time, the Persian chariots charged at the foot

soldiers in the Macedonian centre. But Alexander's archers managed to kill many of the chariot drivers before they reached the soldiers. When a chariot came close, the Macedonians moved sideways and the chariot, which could not turn quickly, went straight through the hole in the line. The chariots were not causing the damage that Darius had hoped for.

On Alexander's left, the Persians broke through the Macedonian defences. But they did not use the situation to their advantage. Instead they went in search of the Persian royal family and tried to free Darius's mother.

Now Alexander took his chance. When the enemy horsemen had rushed to meet the first Macedonian charge, they had left a weak point in the centre of Darius's line. Alexander attacked at this point, passing the elephants and going straight towards the chariot of the Persian king. Alexander, it is said, threw a spear at Darius, but it missed and killed his chariot driver instead. Soon, as at Issus, Darius was rushing from the battlefield in his chariot.

This time Alexander did not want him to escape. He took 2,000 horsemen and hurried after him. But the dust made it difficult to see, and many Persians were trying to follow their king as well. In the confusion, Hephaistion and many of Alexander's other friends were hurt. The Macedonians continued the chase at high speed, but Darius managed to get away.

With the disappearance of their king, the Persian soldiers were soon defeated. As at Issus, enormous numbers of Persians died. The Macedonians too lost many men, and more than a thousand horses died in the battle or from their race to catch Darius.

Alexander marched through rich farmland to Babylon. Its governor came to meet him, and offered him the city without a fight. Alexander entered the city gates in his chariot, riding through streets covered with flowers. The Babylonians, like the Egyptians, had suffered 200 years of unpopular Persian rule, and welcomed a change enthusiastically. Alexander was careful not to follow the Persian habit of insulting the Babylonian gods. He gave gifts to the great god Bel Marduk, and paid for the rebuilding of temples which had been damaged under the Persians.

He spent a few weeks relaxing in the great city with his army. He probably found time to visit the famous Hanging Gardens – a park planted with trees and flowers on many different levels. Like the Mausoleum at Halicarnassus, this was one of the Seven Wonders of the World.

Alexander left Babylon to be ruled by its Persian governor, who had fought against the Macedonians at Gaugamela just a short time before. Many people were surprised at this, thinking that only Greek speakers should rule Alexander's new empire. But later there were other Persian-born governors.

The next great city on Alexander's route east was Susa. The climate there was so hot, it was said, that at midday snakes could not cross the road for fear of being burnt by the sun. But its people gave Alexander a warm welcome, and its great riches made it an attractive destination. After sitting in the royal seat of gold in Darius's palace, Alexander took control of one and a half million kilograms of gold. His financial difficulties at the start of the war were now just a memory.

Then came Persepolis, in the heart of Persia itself. It was natural to expect the Persians to defend their homeland. Alexander led a small group of horsemen and foot soldiers through the mountains to defeat any Persian forces that were defending the mountain roads. The path was steep, narrow and covered in snow. After four days' climb, the Macedonians came to the Persian Gates, a wall of rock in the mountains that marked the entrance to the Persian homeland. As they passed, they were attacked by an enemy army which was much larger than their own small group. Great stones fell on top of them from the mountain heights, and they were shot at on all sides by Persian archers and stone-throwers. Alexander had no choice: he had to order a retreat.

Great stones fell on top of them from the mountain heights.

If Alexander left these Persians undefeated, they could attack his main army, led by his second-in-command, Parmenion, on its way to Persepolis. There was only one hope of success, but it was very dangerous. With half his soldiers, Alexander followed a local guide along a small path used only by animals and their owners. At night, as the wind blew snow in their faces, they ran through the mountains. In the early morning, they rejoined the main path beyond the Persians' position and took the Persians by surprise. With Macedonians in front and behind them, the Persians suffered a terrible defeat. Only a few escaped death.

Finally, in January 330 BC, Persepolis lay undefended. Alexander's soldiers moved through the city, destroying everything and everyone in their path in their search for riches. For many, the long journey from Europe was now well rewarded, as they found extraordinary quantities of gold and silver, jewellery and expensive clothes. But the greatest riches were saved for the Macedonian king. At Persepolis, Alexander found three million kilograms of royal Persian gold. It took 15,000 animals to move it, under Alexander's orders, to Susa.

Alexander chose a new governor for Persepolis – a Persian nobleman whose father had been killed at the Granicus. It seemed that Persepolis was going to receive similar treatment to Babylon and Susa. Then, after a celebratory meal, the Athenian girlfriend of Alexander's friend Ptolemy made a suggestion. Alexander should burn the palace where they were eating, she said, to punish the Persians for burning the Athenian Acropolis many years before. Alexander and his friends agreed, and soon the historic palace of the kings of Persia was in flames.

While Alexander was in Persepolis, Darius and about 10,000 soldiers waited 700 kilometres north in Ecbatana (present-day Hamadan). But when Alexander led his army north, Darius ordered a retreat. First he planned to go far away to Bactria (part of present-day Afghanistan); then he decided to defend the

Caspian Gates, which were much closer. His men were getting annoyed with these changes of plan. Eventually some of them took their king prisoner.

When Alexander heard what had happened, he followed as quickly as he could. Racing through the desert, by day and night, he finally caught up with the Persian soldiers. But their prisoner king was not with them. Tired and thirsty after the long and unsuccessful chase, one of Alexander's officers left the road in search of water. By chance he found a dead body. It was King Darius, murdered by his own men.

Exactly 150 years after King Xerxes's wrongdoings in Athens, the rule of the Persian kings was at an end.

Alexander started wearing the Great King's royal hat and purple-edged clothes, making it clear to the Persians that he was now their Great King. It was a shock for the Macedonians to see their king in Persian clothes. They did not understand why he wanted to look like the enemy. They had won battles that no one had expected them to win, and had become rich beyond their wildest dreams. Now their thoughts turned to home.

To his soldiers' surprise, Alexander made no plans to go back to Europe. Instead he continued to march east, and it is a sign of his extraordinary skills as a leader that his soldiers agreed to follow.

Chapter 8   To the Ends of the Earth

The first aim was to defeat Bessus, one of Darius's murderers. Bessus was now in Bactria, calling himself King of Asia. General Parmenion, Alexander's second-in-command, stayed in Ecbatana with 25,000 men. Cleitus, who had saved Alexander's life at the Battle of the Granicus, was given 6,000 foot soldiers and was told to protect the gold in the city. The other 32,000 soldiers in the Macedonian army marched with Alexander towards Bactria.

The quiet complaints about Alexander's new Persian habits now grew more serious. A group of Macedonians planned to murder their king. Philotas, son of General Parmenion and commander of the Macedonian horsemen, was told about these plans but failed to warn Alexander. When the murder plans were eventually known, Philotas's earlier silence seemed strange. People began to wonder if the murder had been his idea. Philotas was found guilty and killed.

We know that Philotas was a powerful commander who had openly criticized Alexander. We do not know if he was really responsible for the murder plans. Now, though, Alexander had real cause to worry, because Philotas's father, General Parmenion, controlled half of the army at the time of his son's death. It was possible that Parmenion would turn against Alexander in anger at the treatment of his son; it was even possible that Parmenion himself had made the plans to murder Alexander.

Alexander could not afford to wait and see what Parmenion would do. Instead, he organized the murder of this great general, who had been such an important commander in the Macedonian army since the days of Alexander's father, King Philip.

After this, Alexander was very careful. His soldiers' letters to their families were secretly opened. A special group of soldiers was formed of people who had criticized the king. In this way, their dangerous views could not spread to other soldiers who were still loyal to Alexander. In future battles these soldiers fought especially bravely, to prove that they deserved to stay with the army and not be left behind.

After these unpleasant events, the Macedonians marched again towards Bactria. Their route took them straight over the mountains now called the Hindu Kush ('Killer of Hindus'). They climbed 3,000 metres through snow and ice. The army suffered terribly from cold and hunger, and found it difficult to breathe in the thin air. Alexander walked beside his soldiers, helping men

36

who had fallen. The horses suffered most, and were eventually killed and eaten – uncooked, as no firewood could be found under the thick blanket of snow.

Finally they arrived in Bactria. Bessus, who had not expected Alexander's winter crossing of the Hindu Kush, decided to retreat beyond the River Oxus. Most of his soldiers left his army, annoyed that he did not want to stand and fight. Alexander took Bactria's capital city, Bactra, then marched in the footsteps of the retreating Bessus.

Two months before, his men were freezing. Now they had to suffer the terrible heat of a stony desert. They travelled eighty kilometres with almost no water. Alexander shared their suffering, refusing to drink a small cup of water that had been found for him. Soon they reached the River Oxus.

Bessus had destroyed all the bridges and boats, so Alexander ordered his men to fill their leather tent-bags with dried grass and use them to sail across the wide river.

On the far side, they discovered that, like Darius before him, Bessus had been taken prisoner by his own men. Now he was given to Alexander. Alexander sent him back to Ecbatana, where his ears and nose were cut off and he was later killed. This was the traditional Persian punishment for killing a king. To please his new Persian allies, Alexander was punishing the murderer of Darius, who he himself had wanted to kill for so many years.

Alexander now learnt of trouble in the lands that he had already conquered. The people of Sogdiana (present-day Uzbekistan) and Bactria were angry at the way that Alexander's hungry army had taken food and animals from their farms, and started fighting for their independence.

There were sieges in seven cities. Eventually the cities were taken, the enemy soldiers killed, and the women and children sold into slavery. Then news came of trouble at the city of Maracanda (now Samarkand). The Macedonian soldiers there were surrounded by an enemy siege. Alexander had to send an army to help them. But the Scythians on the far side of the River Jaxartes seemed dangerous too. He decided to send only a small force to Maracanda, and to use his main army to defeat the Scythians.

His own battle against the Scythians was successful, and their leaders were soon asking for peace. But in Maracanda, the situation went from bad to worse. The Macedonians were met by enemy horsemen. Without Alexander to lead them, they fought badly, were forced onto a river island and were killed. More than 2,000 men were lost. It was the first real defeat that Alexander's army had suffered.

Alexander spent the summer of 328 BC trying to win back control of Sogdiana. Before he had fully succeeded, a terrible argument started over dinner one night. It was between Alexander and Cleitus, the man who had saved Alexander's life at the Battle of the Granicus. It is possible that the argument was about Alexander's attitude to his older commanders, and to his dead father Philip's memory. Since his visit to Siwah, Alexander believed that he was the son of the god Zeus; perhaps Cleitus thought that Alexander was forgetting the importance of his human father. Certainly many insults were exchanged, and in the end Alexander killed Cleitus with a spear.

In the morning, Alexander felt terrible about losing his temper so violently. He went to his tent and refused to come out for several days. But the murder could not be undone. After this, it seems likely that his relationship with his commanders was different. Cleitus had been killed because he had criticized the king. Nobody else wanted to die for the same reason.

The war, though, started to go better after this. The Sogdians, led by Oxyartes, waited behind steep hilltop defences. They told Alexander that they would only become his allies if he could find soldiers with wings. Instead, he chose 300 soldiers to climb the rockface during the night, just like modern rock climbers. They

Many insults were exchanged.

climbed to a position above the Sogdians. When the Sogdians woke up and saw the rock climbers, they thought for a moment that the Macedonian army really had grown wings. They immediately accepted defeat and were taken prisoner.

Among the prisoners was Oxyartes's beautiful daughter Roxane. Alexander fell in love with her and soon they were married. Politically, this was a good idea too. Oxyartes was a powerful nobleman in Sogdiana, and now he had a strong reason to stay loyal to Alexander.

Others were less loyal. Alexander soon learnt of another plan to murder him. Callisthenes, who was a pupil and close relative of Aristotle and was writing the history of Alexander's heroic adventures, was blamed for the plan and killed.

Beyond Bactria lay India (present-day Pakistan as well as India). Very few Greeks had ever been there, but many strange stories were told of this mysterious land. People said that it was rich in gold, which was dug by enormous insects, and that Indian wool grew on trees. (Cotton was not known in the Mediterranean area at that time.) They said that people lived for 200 years; that there was a tribe of one-footed men; and that to the east of India lay the Eastern Ocean, the edge of the world.

Alexander led his army east into India, more for the adventure than to build an empire. By now, the soldiers were mostly Asian, not European: Asian Greeks from the eastern Mediterranean, and Bactrian, Sogdian and Scythian horsemen and archers. But his most important commanders were his loyal childhood friends, including Perdiccas, Ptolemy and Seleucus. His best friend, Hephaistion, was now his second-in-command.

At first Alexander was surprised by the warm welcome that he was given. A group of Indian kings asked to be his allies and sent him twenty-five elephants to use in battle. But other tribes were not as welcoming. One after the other, their cities were taken and their people killed, until most of the local kings accepted

Alexander as their conqueror. If they did this, they were allowed to continue their rule in peace.

But one king, Porus, preferred to fight. He positioned his army and more than a hundred war elephants on the far bank of the River Hydaspes. Alexander's horses were frightened of elephants, and because it was the rainy season the river was very deep and fast. Alexander could not cross the river and hope for an easy battle.

Every night, Alexander's soldiers pretended to start an attack, shouting the Macedonian war cry 'Alalalalai'. Every night, Porus's men got ready to defend themselves, but as soon as the enemy had got out of bed, Alexander stopped his 'attack'. Soon Porus's men were suffering badly from too little sleep. Porus saw that Alexander had collected enough food to feed his men until the end of the rainy season, and decided that in fact he was not planning to cross the river for many months. He ordered his men not to listen to the nightly Macedonian warcries.

Then Alexander attacked. On a rainy night, he sailed across the river about twenty-five kilometres away from the main armies. His boats landed on an island in the middle of the river, not on the far bank. By the time the mistake was discovered, it was almost light. There was no time to go back to the boats. Instead, Alexander climbed onto the back of his horse Bucephalas, who walked the rest of the crossing with water up to his shoulders. Alexander's soldiers followed, some on horseback and some on foot. Soon the fastest of Porus's soldiers arrived, but their chariots got stuck in mud and they were quickly defeated. Then Alexander marched on Porus's main army, twenty-five kilometres away.

At the front of Porus's battle line were the elephants. Alexander's friends Hephaistion and Perdiccas led horsemen to the far left of the line, beyond the elephants, and Porus's men moved to meet their attack. Then Alexander sent soldiers to attack their right, which was almost undefended. Soon Porus's army was in a state of confusion, and many fighters used their elephants for protection. While Alexander's archers shot at the elephants' drivers, his foot soldiers cut at their legs. The elephants went mad, picking men up and throwing them violently to the ground. Then, frightened and tired, they walked slowly backwards. The battle had ended.

For Alexander, there was just one sad result of the battle. Bucephalas was hurt by Porus's chariots soon after he had crossed the river. A few hours later, he died. Alexander built a new city on the banks of the river and called it Bucephala, in memory of his much-loved horse.

Alexander's army continued east, through the mud of the Punjab's rainy season. When rivers broke their banks, the men had to escape the water in local hilltop villages. The snakes of the area did the same, and many men died from the poisonous bites of snakes hiding in tents, clothes and cooking pots.

They reached the banks of the River Hyphasis, and at this point a local king gave Alexander some unwelcome information. They were still a long way from the Eastern Ocean, which for Greeks meant the edge of the world. To get there, they had to cross the River Ganges, more than five kilometres wide, and fight the powerful King of Maghada and his 4,000 elephants.

Alexander was not especially worried by this news. He had defeated elephants before, and destroyed an empire greater than Maghada's. He called his men together and told them about the adventures and achievements that the future held.

But his men greeted his words with silence. Some of them had marched 18,000 kilometres since they had first arrived in Asia. They had not seen their families for eight long years. And after three terrible months of rain, they were muddy, wet and tired. They did not want to cross the Hyphasis and attack another great empire. They wanted to go home.

Finally, one of the commanders told Alexander their feelings. Soon all the commanders refused to continue east. The first personal defeat in Alexander's life came from his own army. He realized that he had no choice. Many of his men had tears in their eyes as they heard the good news: Alexander was going to lead them home.

In his tent, Alexander was not as happy as his men. His defeat had been very public, and it hurt him greatly. There was a philosopher called Anaxarchus who was travelling with the army. He tried to make Alexander feel better. But according to legend, Alexander cried when Anaxarchus talked about the number of worlds beyond the stars. He explained his tears: 'There are so many worlds, and I have not yet conquered even one.'

Chapter 9   The Last Years

Alexander refused to go back the way that he had come. His taste for adventure was satisfied a little when his men agreed, instead, to build boats. They planned to follow the Hydaspes and Indus rivers south to the Arabian Sea.

The journey started well, but it was difficult to sail so many boats on unfamiliar waters. When the river was too fast, the boats lost control, and many crashed into each other and broke. On one occasion, Alexander had to swim for his life.

Alexander wanted to conquer all the tribes that he passed. The Malloi, who lived in and around the city of Multan, caused him the most trouble. With a small force, Alexander surrounded Multan. Then he led an attack on the city walls. He climbed a ladder and jumped down inside the city. But the enemy managed to break the rest of the Macedonian ladders, and only three of his bodyguards were able to follow him. They fought bravely, but they were attacked on three sides. Other Macedonians arrived as quickly as they could, climbing on each other's shoulders to get to the top of the walls. But when they reached their king, he had a metre-long arrow deep in his chest. They defeated his attackers, then carried him away on his shield, but they had little hope that he would live.

The Malloi were killed – men, women and children – and the other tribes rushed to accept defeat peacefully. But news reached the main army on the river that Alexander was dead. When he finally arrived, not only alive but able to ride and walk, they cried with happiness. They thought that Alexander must truly be protected by the gods.

Alexander's soldiers fought bloody battles against the Brahmins, which brought the total number of Indian dead in the last six months to a quarter of a million. Then the rainy season began again, and there were terrible storms. When they finally reached the Arabian Sea, they gave thanks to the gods. They did not know that the most difficult part of their journey was still ahead of them.

Two hundred years before, the Persian king Cyrus the Great had lost a whole army in the Gedrosian Desert. The desert, now called the Makran, covers 62,000 square kilometres of present-day southern Pakistan and Iran. And their route led across it.

Alexander led a force by land, carrying water for the men who sailed the ships. Alexander's friend Nearchus was in charge of the ships, which brought food for the land army. It was impossible to pull enough food for everyone through the sand of the desert. The sailors and soldiers needed each other.

But the storms of the rainy season delayed the ships after Alexander's army had already entered the desert. Then the local people started fighting, and the ships were unable to take on board all the food that they needed.

In the desert, the sand was deep and the soldiers' legs sank into it. It had been blown into steep mountains and valleys, so every kilometre felt like ten. Occasionally they came to a watering-place. There, thirsty men dived into the water and drank so

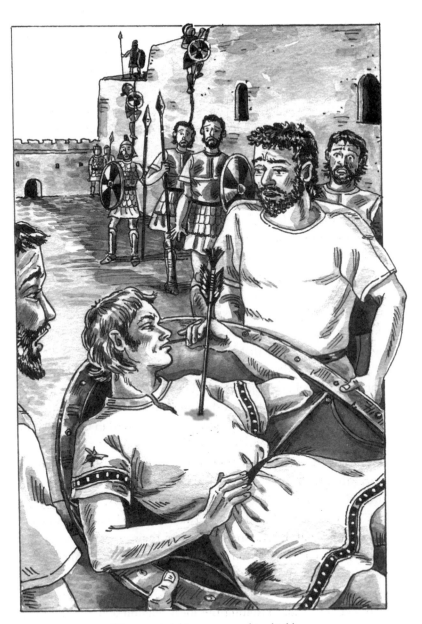

They carried him away on his shield.

greedily that they died. The expected rains came late, and when they did, they arrived very forcefully. Most of the women, children and animals following the army were washed away and killed. The Gedrosian Desert was a hell on earth.

Soon the men started to die of hunger. If they left the army in search of food, they were likely to be killed by poisonous plants or snakes. Then they discovered that their guides had lost their way. Eventually, eight weeks after entering the desert, they came out on the other side. But the desert had proved a much stronger enemy than an army. Tens of thousands of men, women and children had died on the march.

At this time, Nearchus and the ships were only just leaving India. They too were hungry and thirsty on their journey, but Nearchus led them well and they lost few men. Eventually, the ships reached Carmania (in present-day southern Iran), on the far side of the desert, and Alexander was there to welcome them. There were wild celebrations. Sailors and soldiers were together again, and they knew that they were lucky to be alive.

When Alexander had marched over the Hindu Kush, few Persians had believed that he would ever return. Since then, there had been stories that he had died in Multan or in the Gedrosian Desert. They were very surprised when he arrived in Carmania, an easy march from Persepolis.

Few of the conquered lands had stayed loyal in the six years since the Battle of Gaugamela. Some governors had become disloyal as soon as Alexander had left. Others, including the governor of Babylon and Queen Ada of Caria, had died of illness or in battle, and disloyal men had taken their place. Many Greeks and Macedonians had been left as the populations of Alexander's new cities; some had hated their new life and killed their governors. And in Ecbatana, a group of Alexander's generals had behaved very badly, insulting the local religion and attacking the local noblewomen.

Alexander punished his disloyal governors and generals with death. He chose new governors from among his European commanders; too few of his Persian appointments had been a success.

Alexander next planned a great wedding celebration, choosing Persian wives for ninety of his officers. He himself was already married to Roxane, but he decided to follow royal Macedonian tradition and take two more wives: the eldest daughters of Persia's most recent kings, Darius and Artaxerxes. He asked his best friend, Hephaistion, to marry Darius's younger daughter, so that Hephaistion's children could be his own nephews. The weddings were celebrated for five days, in an enormous tent in Susa that had been richly decorated with gold and jewels. Alexander had taken the power of government away from the Persians; now he was including them in his empire in another way.

More and more soldiers from the eastern half of the empire were joining Alexander's army. When he asked his oldest Macedonian soldiers to go home, they felt insulted that he did not need them any more. After ten years in Asia, they now wanted to stay and enjoy the lands that they had conquered. They refused to leave.

The rest of the Macedonian soldiers supported them. 'If you send the old soldiers home, you must send us all,' they told Alexander. But Alexander's decision was final, and he said that they could all go home if they wished; Persians would take their place in his army. Immediately the Macedonians changed their minds. They asked Alexander to forgive them. They wanted him to send the old soldiers home, but allow the rest of them to stay. The problem was solved, and Alexander organized a great dinner to celebrate the friendly relationship between Macedonians and Persians.

Alexander and his friends spent the next few months relaxing and being entertained by theatre performances and sports competitions. But Hephaistion caught a fever, became ill and died. His death was a terrible shock to his lifelong friend and king. For many weeks he was unable to think about anything else.

Slowly Alexander returned to his usual business. He planned to send ships and a land army around the coast of Arabia from Persia to Egypt. Other ships were going to check if the Caspian Sea was part of a northern ocean or joined the Black Sea; although its southern coast was part of the empire, no one seemed to know at that time that the Caspian Sea was actually a lake.

But in Babylon, Alexander suddenly became ill. Possibly he had been poisoned by his officers; probably he had caught a disease carried by insects while he was travelling on Babylon's waterways. He had a high fever, and after a week he could not talk. On the tenth day, his court and army were given the unthinkable news: Alexander the Great was dead.

Chapter 10   After Alexander

Although Alexander's achievements had spread Greek customs far into Asia, the Greeks in Europe were pleased about his death and decided to fight for their independence. To them, he was still a foreigner. But the Persians, who had lost an empire and hundreds of thousands of men because of Alexander, were very upset when they heard that he had died. King Darius's mother, who had become Alexander's prisoner after the Battle of Issus, stopped eating when she heard the news, and was dead herself five days later. Alexander had become the Persians' Great King, whose rule followed the traditions of the past. He had been their friend as well as their conqueror. And, rightly, they feared a future without him.

Alexander died with no close male relative except his brother Arrhidaeus, who had learning difficulties. But Roxane, Alexander's first wife, was soon going to have a baby. Alexander's friends decided to make the unborn child the next king, if the baby was a boy. Alexander's friend Perdiccas, who had been his second-in-command after the death of Hephaistion and had royal blood himself, would rule until the baby grew up.

But the common soldiers wanted Arrhidaeus as their king, as he was fully Macedonian and Roxane's baby had Asian blood. Less than a week after Alexander's death, fighting began. It was only stopped when Perdiccas ordered the death of thirty of the soldiers' leaders and they were thrown to the elephants. It was agreed that rule would be shared between Roxane's baby and Arrhidaeus.

There were many years of confusion in the empire that Alexander had built. The story of Alexander's dead body is typical of the times. It was believed that the body's final resting place would bring good luck to the local people. Perdiccas ordered his men to take it from Babylon to Macedonia in a box of gold. But Ptolemy, who had been a close friend of Alexander and had recently made himself king of an independent Egypt, took the body in secret to Egyptian Alexandria, where it stayed for hundreds of years.

During the years after Alexander's death, Roxane poisoned Alexander's other wives to protect the power of her baby son, also called Alexander. Perdiccas ruled for a short time, until he was murdered by his bodyguards. Alexander's most loyal commanders all wanted power for themselves, and they were willing to murder people to get it.

Antipater was the general who had controlled the Macedonian army in Europe while Alexander was in Asia. When Antipater died of old age, his son Cassander took control of Macedonia. Alexander's mother, Olympias, was officially in charge of Macedonia and tried to protect her power. She murdered King Arrhidaeus, her husband's son and Alexander's half-brother, and defended herself in the Macedonian town of Pydna. But Cassander put the town under siege. After nine months she had no food, and she died proudly. Cassander then killed Roxane and her son, who were visiting Greece, and made himself King of Macedonia.

The Macedonians soon sold the lands that Alexander had conquered in India; they received 500 elephants for them. Many years later, these lands were reconquered by the Greek-speaking kings of Bactria, whose family had been started by one of Alexander's Macedonian governors.

After years of fighting, two of Alexander's commanders controlled most of his empire. Ptolemy was King of Egypt and Seleucus king of the Asian empire. The families of both men stayed in power until their lands were conquered by the Romans in the first century BC.

All over Alexander's empire, Greek-style cities had been built. Their populations were mostly European, and became perhaps more Greek in their habits as the years passed. In some areas, they preferred to marry their sister, niece or granddaughter than to join their family with the foreigners that surrounded them. Each city had a gymnasium, and held sporting competitions and theatre performances. In Afghanistan, buildings and works of art have been discovered which copied exactly the artistic styles of Greece. The works of Homer, Plato and Aristotle were read and enjoyed in India and even across the sea in Sri Lanka.

The greatest of Alexander's new cities was Alexandria, the capital of Egypt under the Ptolemaic kings. While many parts of Alexander's empire suffered from continued fighting, Egypt lived in peace and grew in power. Its economy was very successful; from Alexandria, ships took paper, medicines, jewellery and art all over the known world.

The Ptolemaic kings mixed Greek customs with Egyptian traditions, and built temples to both Greek and Egyptian gods. They were very interested in literature, philosophy and science, and invited the most famous writers of their age to live in Alexandria. Out of this collection of great men grew a great idea:

a library that brought together all Greek knowledge and included every book that had ever been written. At its largest, this library held 50,000 books – not a lot compared to the great modern libraries, but in a world before printing machines this was an extraordinary number.

Among these books was a growing collection of histories of Alexander's life. Some of them were interested in the facts; others told romantic stories that were completely untrue. They said that he and his warhorse Bucephalas each had two horns on their heads. They told of strange flying machines, a Valley of Diamonds, and the secret of immortality. Alexander's legend was told from Iceland to China; in death he travelled far beyond the borders of his own empire.

Over the years, interest in Alexander has been shown in many different ways. He appears in the *Book of Daniel*, which was written in Hebrew in the second century BC and now forms part of the Christian Bible. He was the hero of Julius Caesar, Rome's greatest general. The Italian artist Michelangelo created a square in Rome to look like Alexander's famous shield. The French ruler Napoleon used to read about Alexander in bed every night. In the early 1900s, tribal kings in Afghanistan still went into battle carrying a red flag which, according to their legends, had belonged to Alexander. And in 2004, Alexander's extraordinary story was brought to life in a $155 million Hollywood film. It starred Colin Farrell as Alexander and was watched in cinemas all around the world. Alexander the Great may be more famous in the twenty-first century than he ever was.

ACTIVITIES

Chapter 1

Before you read

1 What do you know about Alexander the Great? List five facts. Then read the Introduction to the book.

2 What do you know about the Greeks who lived more than 2,000 years ago? Look at the Word List at the back of the book. Then discuss what you know about:
   a their heroes, gods and legends
   b their temples
   c their philosophy and literature
   d their political life
   e their wars
   f their sports

While you read

3 Write the name of:
   a a Persian king ....
   b a democratic Greek city-state ....
   c the king of the Greek gods ....
   d a religious centre in Greece ....
   e a city that was famous for sport ....
   f the capital city of Macedonia ....

After you read

4 Answer these questions.
   a Did many Greek people live outside the modern-day country of Greece?
   b Had the Greeks and the Persians ever fought before the time of Alexander the Great?
   c Were the different Greek states normally at peace with each other?
   d What two differences were there between the people of southern Greece and the Macedonians?

Chapter 2

Before you read

5 You are going to read about Alexander's early life. Guess which of these he did before he was eighteen:

  a travelled to Persia
  b had lessons with his friends
  c hunted with dogs
  d rode horses
  e fought in battles
  f got married

6 Discuss this question with other students:
  Are people born great, or do their experiences in childhood make them great?

While you read

7 Match the names with their relationship to Alexander.

a	Philip	**i**	his father's new wife
b	Olympias	**ii**	his father
c	Bucephalas	**iii**	his best friend
d	Aristotle	**iv**	his horse
e	Hephaistion	**v**	his teacher
f	Eurydice	**vi**	his mother

After you read

8 What were Philip's achievements as ruler of Macedonia?

9 Discuss whether you would like Aristotle as your teacher.

10 Why did these people have to leave Macedonia?
  a Olympias   **b** Alexander's friends

11 If someone paid the bodyguard to kill Philip, who do you think that person was? Discuss the possible guilty people and their reasons.

12 Work with another student. You are both important people in the Macedonian government and you need to choose a new king. Talk about Alexander's character and experience. Would he be a good king?

Chapters 3–4

Before you read

13 You are going to read about Alexander's first years as king. Guess which of these he did:

   a punished the person who ordered his father's death

   b killed members of his own family

   c fought the Greeks

   d fought the Persians

While you read

14 Are these sentences true (T) or false (F)?

   a Alexander was the only possible king of Macedonia
      after the death of his father. .....

   b Neighbouring Greek cities voted to destroy Thebes. .....

   c Alexander met Achilles at Troy. .....

   d Memnon was Alexander's second-in-command. .....

   e There were more Greeks in the Persian army than in
      Alexander's army. .....

   f Queen Ada fought against Alexander at Halicarnassus. .....

After you read

15 What happened at these places?

   a Thessaly

   b Troy

   c the River Granicus

   d Gordium

16 Discuss why Achilles was Alexander's favourite hero from Greek legend.

17 Work with another student. Imagine that you are Greek people living at the time of Alexander. Have a discussion and give reasons for your opinions.

   Student A: You think Alexander is a great king and a hero.

   Student B: You think Alexander is a terrible king and a bloodthirsty murderer.

Chapters 5–6

Before you read

18 Discuss these questions. If you cannot answer them, find information in books or on the Internet.

   a In Chapter 5, Alexander fights against Darius III, king of Persia. Where was Persia? What do you know about the Persians, their empire and their kings?

   b In Chapter 6, Alexander goes to Egypt. What do you know about the history of Egypt?

19 What dangers do people meet when they travel across a desert?

While you read

20 Match the questions with the answers.

   Where did Alexander:

   a nearly die of a fever?   **i** Libya

   b see King Darius for the first time?   **ii** Tarsus

   c build a road across the sea?   **iii** Issus

   d build a new city?   **iv** Egypt

   e nearly die in the desert?   **v** Tyre

After you read

21 Which army, Alexander's or Darius's:

   a was led by Memnon on the Greek islands?

   b was bigger?

   c had more women, children and servants with it?

   d won the Battle of Issus?

22 Which of these people and gods did Alexander behave cruelly to?

   a his doctor, Philip

   b King Darius's wife and mother

   c the people of Tyre

   d King Batis of Gaza

   e the Egyptian gods

23 Why did Alexander go to Siwah? In what way was he different after his visit there?

Chapter 7

Before you read

24 In this chapter there is another big battle between the armies of
Alexander and Darius. Guess the answers to these questions.
   a Who wins the battle?
   b How does Alexander behave towards Persian people and
buildings after the battle?
   c What happens to King Darius?

While you read

25 Complete the sentences.
   a Alexander and Darius fought again at the great Battle of
   ....
   b The people of .... were happy to welcome Alexander
   to their city.
   c There was .... on the ground when Alexander fought
   the Persians in the mountains near Persepolis.
   d At Persepolis, Alexander found three million kilograms of
   ....
   e Alexander .... the palace at Persepolis.
   f The Persians took .... prisoner and then killed him.

After you read

26 At Gaugamela, why did Alexander leave the battlefield before the
end of the battle?

27 Work with another student. Imagine that you are two of Darius's
soldiers.
   Student A: You are angry about your king's mistakes. Tell your
   friend why Darius deserves to die.
   Student B: You are loyal to your king. Explain why you do not
   want him to be killed.

28 Discuss the advantages and disadvantages of Alexander's decision
to wear Persian clothes and to give important political appointments
to Persian people.

Chapter 8

Before you read

29 Alexander marched east through present-day Afghanistan, Pakistan and India. Do you think anyone defeated him in that time? Why did he eventually turn back?

While you read

30 Tick ✓ the problems that Alexander faced in this chapter.

a	illness	.....	**f** plans to kill him	.....
b	the death of his mother	.....	**g** a forest fire	.....
c	very cold weather	.....	**h** hungry soldiers	.....
d	very hot weather	.....	**i** elephants	.....
e	very wet weather	.....	**j** snakes	.....

After you read

31 Who were they? What happened to them in this chapter?

    a Bessus **b** Parmenion **c** Roxane **d** Bucephalas

32 How did Alexander:

    a find out which of his soldiers were disloyal?

    b cross the River Oxus?

    c make a surprise attack on Porus's army?

33 Imagine that you are Alexander's court historians. You know that Alexander only wants you to write about his successes and the good things in his life. Discuss which of these people and places to include in your history, and which to leave out.

Philotas   the Hindu Kush   Maracanda   Cleitus   Oxyartes
Callisthenes   Porus

34 Work with another student. Imagine that you are beside the River Hyphasis in India. Act out this conversation.

    Student A: You are one of Alexander's commanders. Explain (politely!) why you and your soldiers are angry with him and why you want to go home.

    Student B: You are Alexander. Give reasons for your past behaviour and explain why you think the army should continue east.

Chapters 9–10

Before you read

35 Discuss these questions. If you do not know the answers, guess.

    a How did Alexander die?

    b What happened to his empire after his death?

While you read

36 Put these events in the correct order, 1–6.

    a Tens of thousands of Alexander's soldiers died.   .....

    b The Romans conquered much of Alexander's empire.   .....

    c Hephaistion died.   .....

    d Alexander was shot with an arrow.   .....

    e Alexander and Roxane's baby was born.   .....

    f Alexander died.   .....

After you read

37 Why does the book describe the Gedrosian Desert as a 'hell on earth'?

38 Was the news that Alexander was leaving India and returning to Persia good news or bad news for these people? Why/Why not?

    a the Indians   **b** the rulers of Caria and Babylon

39 Work with another student. Imagine that you are officers in Alexander's army. You have been told that you will be married to Persian women. Have a discussion and give reasons for your opinions.

    Student A: You are pleased. You think the marriage will be a good thing for you and for Macedonia.

    Student B: You are angry. You think the marriage is a terrible idea.

40 Which of these people were still alive many years after Alexander's death? What happened to the others?

    a Ptolemy   **b** Roxane   **c** Hephaistion

    d Perdiccas   **e** Seleucus   **f** Olympias

41 Imagine that Alexander died at sixty-two, not at thirty-two. Discuss how history might be different.